ARCHITECTURE

YESTERDAY'S SCIENCE
TODAY'S TECHNOLOGY
SCIENCE ACTIVITIES

ARCHITECTURE

ROBERT GARDNER

DRAWINGS BY DORIS ETTLINGER

TWENTY-FIRST CENTURY BOOKS

A DIVISION OF HENRY HOLT AND COMPANY / NEW YORK

Twenty-First Century Books
A Division of Henry Holt and Company, Inc.
115 West 18th Street
New York, NY 10011

Henry Holt® and colophon are trademarks of
Henry Holt and Company, Inc.
Publishers since 1866

Published in Canada by Fitzhenry & Whiteside Ltd.
195 Allstate Parkway, Markham, Ontario L3R 4T8

Library of Congress Cataloging-in-Publication Data
Gardner, Robert, 1929–
Architecture / Robert Gardner.—1st ed.
p.   cm.—(Yesterday's science, today's technology)
Includes index.
1. Structural engineering—Experiments—Juvenile literature.
2. Buildings—Experiments—Juvenile literature.
3. Architecture—Experiments—Juvenile literature.
[1. Structural engineering—Experiments   2. Buildings—Experiments.
3. Architecture—Experiments.]   I. Title   II. Series: Gardner, Robert, 1929-
Yesterday's science, today's technology.
TA634.G37   1994
721—dc20   94–21423
                                                        CIP
                                                        AC
ISBN 0-8050-2855-2
First Edition—1994

Printed in the United States of America
All first editions are printed on acid-free paper ∞.

1   3   5   7   9   10   8   6   4   2

CONTENTS

INTRODUCTION

Animals as different as bees and beavers build rather elaborate dwellings without a blueprint to guide them. The same is true of some dwellings built in primitive human cultures. In the case of insects, their architectural skills appear to be carried in their genes. The same may also be true of mammals such as beavers, although they do seem to be adaptable and capable of learning and planning in ways that we don't understand. Humans learned to build huts from their ancestors or by trial and error. But the ability to draw plans, use science and mathematics to calculate the forces needed to make a building stand, and develop and utilize new building techniques and technologies is limited to humans.

Architecture is the designing and construction of buildings. Vitruvius, an early Roman architect, first expressed a fundamental architectural principle: A building should be a combination of function, sound construction, and beauty. To fulfill this principle, an architect must have artistic skills and sensitivity as well as a firm knowledge of mathematics and other sciences to design buildings that are both long lasting and attractive. Schools dedicated to the study of architecture and the training of professional architects did not exist before the nineteenth century, but people with architectural skills must have lived thousands of years ago. The massive stone pillars and beams at Stonehenge in England, the Egyptian pyramids, and the buildings of classical Greece and Rome reveal early architectural styles and building skills that required careful planning and a grasp of basic scientific principles. Without detailed plans and ingenious methods of construction, these structures could never have been built.

In this book you will have an opportunity to investigate some of the science and technology associated with architecture. You will learn, through your reading and in hands-on fashion, some of the basic principles of architecture. Each chapter contains a number of activities designed to enhance your understanding of the subject. You will find an ✖ beside a few activities. The ✖ indicates that you should ask an adult to help you because the activity may involve an action or the use of something that might be dangerous. Be sure to find adult help before attempting activities marked in this way.

Other activities, which are preceded by a ★, might serve as starting points for a science fair project. Bear in mind, however, that judges at such contests are looking for original ideas and creative thinking. Projects copied from a book are not likely to impress anyone. However, you may find that one or more of the activities in this book will stimulate a project or experiment of your own design that will lead you to the winner's circle at your school's next science or invention fair.

1

EARLY ARCHITECTURE

Our earliest ancestors, like many primitive peoples today, were no-
mads who found shelter in caves or in huts built from small trees,
branches, leaves, reeds, or animal hides. With the development of
agriculture, more permanent dwellings were constructed. The materials used for building depended on what was available locally. In
the Middle East, bricks were made from wet, clay-rich soil that was
mixed with chaff and straw and molded in precut forms. The damp
bricks were then left in the sun to dry and harden. Bricks made from
clay heated in kilns appeared first in the Middle East after 4000 B.C.

In China, the primary building material was wood. The
Egyptians used stones in public buildings, but ordinary dwellings
were made of sun-dried bricks. A common method of construction, found in many places, was cobwork. Earth was rammed between parallel boards to form large "bricks" of earth. When the soil
dried, it was coated with plaster of paris to repel water. A good
portion of the Great Wall of China was built this way and has lasted
for 23 centuries.

These methods of construction were probably developed
through trial and error. There is no evidence that science played a
significant role in early architecture until the building of the pyramids during the third millennium B.C. and Stonehenge, which was
probably built between 2100 and 1500 B.C.

Stonehenge is an ancient monument in southwestern England.

BUILDING A PRIMITIVE DWELLING

MATERIALS

- *natural materials such as small trees, branches, leaves, vines, stones, soil, etc.*

Under adult supervision, pretend that you and a friend are early humans building a small hut to protect you from the sun's intense heat and keep you dry on rainy days. Since you are early humans, none of the technology of your descendants, such as hammers, saws, nails, and concrete, is available. You have access only to natural materials.

Stones weighing many tons were somehow raised to great heights in constructions found in Egypt, Greece, and Rome. The Great Pyramid of Cheops in Egypt rises to almost 150 m (500 ft) and is built of stones that weigh several tons each. The Parthenon in Greece, erected in the fifth century B.C., has columns 10 m (33 ft) high. A column consists of 11 0.9-m (3-ft) high drums each weighing eight tons. There is no way that humans could lift such stones with their muscles. To build such structures, early architects and builders must have had a basic understanding of the principles of simple machines. Where can you find more recently built buildings that resemble the Parthenon?

Some believe earthen ramps served as inclined planes, and levers were used to slide the stones along the inclines and into place. Activity 2 will show you how with simple machines a small force can lift a heavy weight.

The Great Pyramid of Cheops in Egypt contains more than 2 million large blocks.

SIMPLE MACHINES IN ARCHITECTURE

MATERIALS

- *two 11-L (12-qt) pails*
- *strong board (a 2 by 6 is good) about 1.8–2 m (5–6 ft) long*
- *sand*
- *shovel*
- *carpenter's ruler*
- *round stick or broom handle*
- *large toy truck that weighs 0.45 kg (1 lb) or more*
- *strong rubber band*
- *string*
- *paper clip*
- *ruler*
- *crank-type pencil sharpener*
- *soft stick*
- *masking tape*
- *measuring cup*
- *water*

A lever is a simple machine. One end of a lever, such as a board, can be used to lift a heavy weight when a much smaller force is applied at the other end. To see how this works, center your strong board on a stick of wood or broom handle as shown in Figure 1a. Place a pail full of sand on one end of the board. Another pail of sand on the opposite end of the board should balance the board. If it doesn't quite balance, add or subtract a little sand.

Carefully remove the pail from one end of the board. Push on that end to raise the pail at the opposite end. You can feel how much push is needed to lift the pail of sand.

The point about which a lever rotates is called the fulcrum. In your setup the stick is the fulcrum and the board is

pails of sand

strong board
(lever)

a.

stick
(fulcrum)

b.

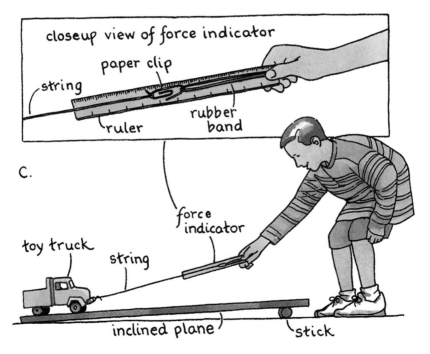

closeup view of force indicator

paper clip

string

ruler

rubber
band

c.

force
indicator

toy truck

string

inclined plane

stick

Figure 1: a. A balanced beam with a fulcrum at the middle of
the lever. b. Making work easier with a lever. c. Making work
easier with an inclined plane.

the lever. Move the fulcrum until it is about 30 cm (1 ft) from the pail of sand (see Figure 1b). Again, push on the opposite end of the lever. What has happened to the force needed to raise the pail of sand? What happens to the force needed to lift the sand as the fulcrum is moved closer to the center of the board? How can you use a lever to lift a 45-kg (100-lb) weight with a 9-kg (20-lb) force?

An inclined plane was probably used to raise heavy stones in building the pyramids. To see how an inclined plane reduces the force needed to lift something, you can use the board you used before as an inclined plane (see Figure 1c). Place one end of the board on the stick that you used before as a fulcrum. Place a toy truck on the board and pull it with a rubber band attached to a string through a paper clip as shown. The amount the rubber band stretches, as measured by a ruler, indicates the force needed to pull the truck along the inclined plane.

To see why early builders probably placed heavy stones on rollers, turn the truck over so that it is no longer on wheels. How does the force needed to move the truck now compare with the force needed when the truck was on wheels?

Next, hang the toy truck from the rubber band. Now the truck's weight is the force stretching the rubber band. How does the truck's weight compare with the force needed to pull it up the inclined plane? If you make the inclined plane steeper, what happens to the force needed to pull the truck along the board? What is the steepest angle you can have between the board and the floor? How much will the rubber band stretch at this angle?

A third simple machine used in early construction was the wheel and axle, or windlass. It was used to lift stones from a quarry or to the top of a wall or roof. A crank-type pencil sharpener (see Figure 2) is basically a wheel and axle. To see how it can be used to reduce the force needed to raise a weight, remove the cover that holds the pencil shavings. Into

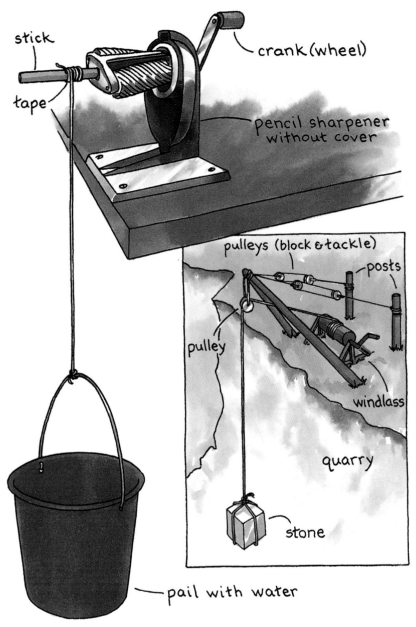

stick

crank (wheel)

tape

pencil sharpener
without cover

pulleys (block & tackle)

posts

pulley

windlass

quarry

stone

pail with water

Figure 2. A windlass is a simple machine used to reduce the force needed to lift a weight.

the opening where you normally put a pencil, insert instead a soft stick slightly larger than the opening to make a tight fit. The stick will serve as the axle. The pencil sharpener's handle will serve as the wheel (crank).

Use masking tape to attach one end of a string to the axle. Connect the other end of the string to a pail that contains about 0.5 L (1 pt) of water as shown in Figure 2. Lift the pail by pulling upward on the string with your hand. Then raise the pail by turning the crank. How does the force needed to turn the crank compare with the weight of the pail and water?

2

FROM POINT TO SPACE, FROM PLANS TO BUILDING

Architects' ideas are expressed in plans. The fundamental element in a plan is a point. Ideally a point has no dimensions (no length, width, or height), but in practice we represent a point with a dot. If a point is extended (see Figure 3a), we obtain a line that can be measured. In practice, we use a pencil to "drag" a dot to make a line. If a line is moved in a direction perpendicular to itself, it sweeps out a plane—a flat surface—which has an area that can be measured. If the line moves a distance equal to its own length, the area of the figure it sweeps out is called a square. If moved a distance other than its length, the area is called a rectangle. The size of the area is determined by the number of unit squares that will fit onto the surface. For example, a square 5 cm (2 in.) on a side has an area of 25 cm^2 (4 in.^{2}) as shown in Figure 3b.

If a square is moved in a direction perpendicular to its surface (see Figure 3c), it sweeps out a volume—a space. If the distance the square is moved equals the length of the square, the volume is called a cube. If moved any other distance, the space swept out is called a rectangular solid. The volume of the space can be determined by figuring out how many unit cubes will fit into it. For example, a cube 5 cm (2 in.) on any given side contains 125 cm^3 (8 in.^{3}) (see Figure 3d).

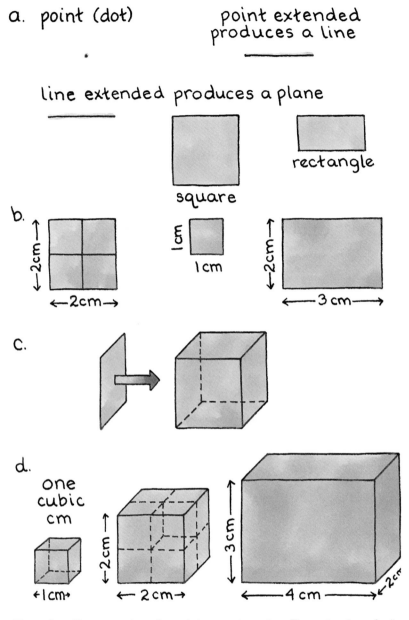

a. point (dot)   point extended
                      produces a line

line extended produces a plane

rectangle

square

b.

← 2cm →   ←2cm→

1 cm
1 cm

← 2cm →   ←—3 cm—→

c.

d.

one
cubic
cm

← 1 cm →   ← 2cm →   ←— 4 cm —→
← 2 cm   3 cm   2 cm

Figure 3: a. The extension of a point generates a line. The extension of a line perpendicular to the line itself sweeps out a plane or surface. b. The area of a surface is equal to the number of unit squares it encloses. A square one cm on a side has an area of one square cm. A square two cm on a side encloses four square cm. What is the area of the rectangle shown? c. An extended surface sweeps out a space. d. A cube two cm on a side encloses eight cubic cm. What is the volume of the figure shown?

An architect must be able to draw and visualize areas and volumes. Activity 3 will help you to understand the kind of thinking architects do.

REPRESENTATIONS OF LENGTHS, AREAS, AND VOLUMES

MATERIALS
- *paper*
- *dark crayon*
- *ruler*
- *scissors*
- *modeling clay*

Use a dark crayon to make a dot on a sheet of paper. Use the crayon and a ruler to extend the point to make a line 5 cm (2 in.) long. Next, remove the paper on the crayon, break the crayon so it is exactly 5 cm (2 in.) long, and place it on the line you have drawn. Let the crayon represent the line. (A rather fat line to be sure!) To sweep out a plane, press down on the crayon and drag it 5 cm (2 in.) across the paper as shown in Figure 4a. You now have a square surface 5 cm (2 in.) on a side. What is the area of the square?

Use scissors to cut out the colored square. If you move the square along a line perpendicular to its surface, you will sweep out a volume. If you move it 5 cm (2 in.), how much volume will you sweep out? Of course, you cannot see this volume because air is invisible, but the space will be visible if you fill it with something. On top of the colored square use modeling clay to build a cube 5 cm (2 in.) high (see Figure 4b). What is the shape of the clay structure? What is its volume in cubic centimeters (cubic inches)?

a.

dot •

dot extended to make 5cm line _____

crayon representing line

press on crayon and pull to sweep
out plane 5cm wide to pro-
duce dark plane shown below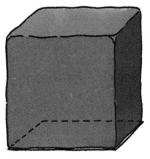

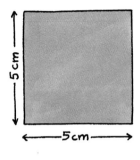

5 cm

←——5cm——→

b. clay cube covering square

c.

line rotated about
a fixed point

Figure 4: a. A crayon is used to draw a dot, extend the dot to a line, and sweep out an area with the line. b. Modeling clay is used to extend the square five cm on a side through a height of five cm. c. One end of a line is fixed and the other end is moved. What is the shape of the surface swept out by the line?

Using the same piece of crayon, keep one end in place while you move the other end all the way around to its starting point (see Figure 4c). What is the shape of the plane swept out by the line? Now imagine that plane moving in a direction perpendicular to its surface. What will be the shape of the volume it sweeps out?

Draw a diagonal across a rectangle as shown in Figure 5a. What is the shape of each half of the rectangle? If that surface is turned about one side, which is kept fixed as shown in Figure 5b, what will be the shape of the volume swept out? If the surface generated by moving a line fixed at one end (see Figure 4c) is rotated about an axis along its diameter (see Figure 5c), what will be the shape of the volume it sweeps out?

As you have seen, the basic plane shapes—square, circle, and triangle—can be moved to sweep out the basic three-dimensional shapes—cubes, rectangular solids, cylinders, spheres, and cones. Figure 5d shows how different plane figures can be combined to form other figures and enclose various shaped spaces. What additional shaped planes and solids can you visualize using the basic plane shapes? Which of them have you seen in buildings?

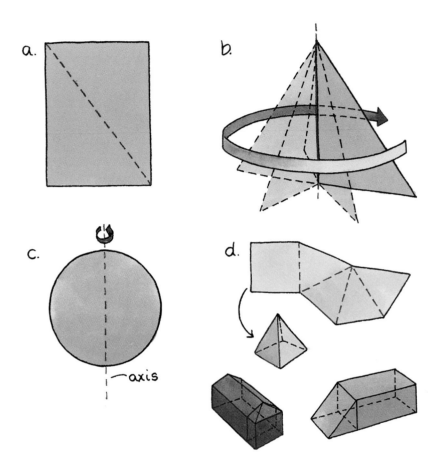

a.

b.

c.

⌇axis

d.

Figure 5: a. A rectangle cut in half by its diagonal. b. The half rectangle being turned about one side to sweep out a volume. c. A circle is rotated about its axis (diameter). What is the shape of the volume it sweeps out? d. Various planes and shapes produced by combinations of basic plane figures.

MAKING PLANS

MATERIALS

- *paper*
- *metric ruler*
- *sharp pencil*
- *T square or other right angle*
- *measuring tape or carpenter's ruler*

Before a building is constructed, an architect draws plans of it. One of the plans is a floor plan like the one shown in Figure 6. All the lengths and widths shown in the plan are scaled reductions of the actual dimensions. In the plan shown, the scale is 1:100; that is, 1 cm on the drawing represents 100 cm of length in the actual building.

According to the plan, what will be the length of the building? Its width? What are the dimensions of each room?

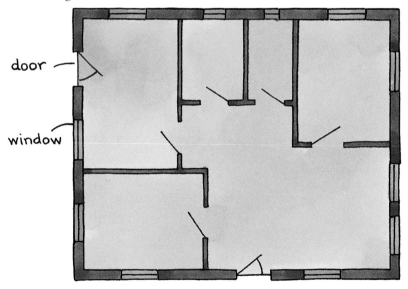

scale 1 cm = 100 cm

Figure 6. A simple floor plan.

23

How wide are the windows? How wide are the doors? How thick are the walls?

Make a floor plan of your own home, apartment, or school. How can you find the thickness of the walls without drilling holes? Draw a plan of the outside walls and roof of your home.

Draw a floor plan of your "dream" house. Make a scaled drawing of the sides of your dream house as seen from the outside. Make a sketch of the site of your dream home as an artist might draw it. Include shrubs, trees, flowers, walks, and so on. You can find samples of such drawings in magazines at your local library. What additional drawings would be required before a builder could construct your home?

Building, Mathematics, and Gravity

The pyramids are very large, but they have very little space inside. Pyramids are almost solid throughout—one stone piled on another

The Parthenon in Greece was built in the fifth century B.C.

like a mountain. Stones can withstand compression—the forces that squeeze material together (see Figure 7a). As a result, it is possible to build huge solid structures from stone. On the other hand, forces of tension—forces that tend to pull material apart (see Figure 7b)—readily break stone. Opposing forces that do not act along the same line are called shear forces (see Figure 7c).

The Greeks who built the Parthenon were interested in providing not a simple monument, like the pyramids, but a structure that

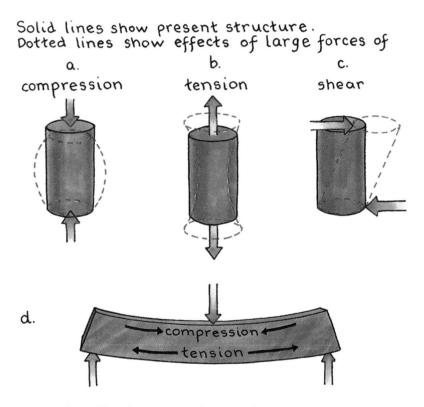

Figure 7: a. Compression forces tend to squeeze matter together. b. Tension forces tend to pull matter apart. c. Shear forces are opposing forces that do not act along the same line. d. When a beam is bent, the top of the beam is subject to compression forces—the material is pushed together. The bottom of the beam is subject to tension because the material is stretched. Wood and steel can stretch but stone cannot.

enclosed a space where people might gather. As you can see, their buildings had many closely spaced stone columns (pillars). The pillars are close together because horizontal stone beams break if they span too great a distance. The lower side of a beam, as you can see from Figure 7d, is subject to forces of tension when it bends. If the beam is made of stone, which lacks tensile strength (ability to withstand tension), it will break quite readily if bent by its own weight or the weight of other stones piled on it.

Beams in buildings and bridges are subject to forces of compression and tension because they have to support weight across a span. If you try to support a heavy porch with widely spaced upright 2 by 4s (2 in. by 4 in. boards), the boards will bend and perhaps break. Either the 2 by 4s will have to be placed closer together or thicker supports will be required. Placing more uprights closer together may make entry difficult and spoil the appearance of the porch; the appearance may be more pleasing if you use more widely spaced 4 by 4s, which will support twice as much weight as 2 by 4s.

★ ACTIVITY 5

TESTING FLOORS AND BRIDGES

MATERIALS
- *two meter sticks or yardsticks*
- *two tables*
- *string*
- *plastic pail*
- *ruler*
- *water*
- *measuring cup*

Architects who design bridges and buildings must consider a number of factors to be certain the beams, decks, and floors can support the weight they must carry. Some of these factors are the length of the span, the building material used, the width of the beams and boards, and the weight that must be supported. What other factors should be considered?

To see how the length of the span affects a floor or bridge, place a meter stick or yardstick between two tables as shown in Figure 8a. Set the edges of the tables 60 cm (2 ft) apart so that the 20-cm (or 6-in.) and 80-cm (or 30-in.) markings on the meter stick (or yardstick) are even with the table edges. Use a string to hang a plastic pail from the middle of the stick. Lay a straight board or another stick beside the one that spans the tables so you can use a ruler to measure how much the middle of the stick bends. Pour water into the pail half a cupful at a time until the stick is 2.5 cm (1 in.) lower at its midpoint.

Move the tables together until the span is 30 cm (or 1 ft) and the 35-cm (or 12-in.) and 65-cm (or 24-in.) marks on the stick line up with the table edges. How much does the stick bend when the span is halved? Does halving the span halve the bending?

Move the tables until the span is again 60 cm (2 ft). Have a friend support the stick so it is on its narrow rather than its wide edge as shown in Figure 8b. Hang the pail with the same maximum amount of water as before at the middle of the stick. How much does the stick bend when its narrow edge extends across the span? How is the bending of a cantilevered beam (a beam supported by only one end) affected by the weight it must support (see Figure 8c)? By the length it extends beyond its support?

In a basement, you can see the long joists that support the floor and span the space across the foundation. Sometimes a thick beam perpendicular to the joists supports them near their middle. Do the joists lie flat or are they turned up on their narrow edge? Can you explain why?

Design an experiment to see how the thickness of a beam affects its bending.

Design an experiment to see how the width of a beam affects the amount it bends.

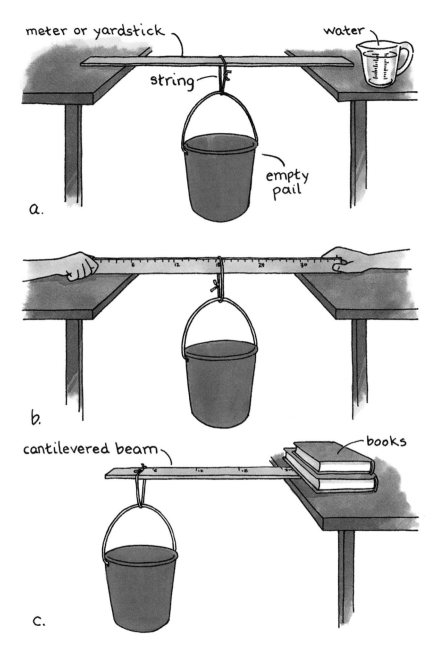

Figure 8: a. A flat yardstick is placed across a span. How much does it bend when weight is added to it? b. How does turning the yardstick onto its narrow side affect the amount it bends? c. How is a cantilevered beam affected by weight? By length?

Design an experiment to see how bending is affected by the material used to span the gap. You might try different kinds of wood, plastic, and various metals.

Bending, Compression, Tension, and I Beams

As you have seen, a weight-supporting beam has forces of compression acting along its top and forces of tension acting along its bottom (see Figure 9a). The middle of the beam does little more than separate top and bottom. For that reason, and to reduce costs, the steel beams used in heavy construction are I-shaped (or H-shaped). The top and bottom of an I beam are wide to counter the forces of compression and tension, but the middle part of the beam is narrow (see Figure 9b).

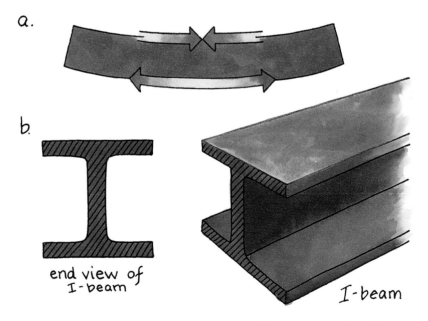

a.

b.

end view of
I-beam

I-beam

Figure 9: a. The top of a beam is subject to compression; the bottom is subject to tension. b. An I beam provides strength where the forces of compression and tension are greatest.

TESTING THE COMPRESSION AND TENSILE
STRENGTH OF PAPER

MATERIALS

- *typing or computer paper*
- *tape*
- *spring-type bathroom scale*
- *books*
- *paper and plastic soda straws*
- *pail*
- *wood dowel*
- *soft pad*
- *sink*
- *different brands of paper towels*
- *different kinds of paper, such as wrapping, writing, newspaper, and facial tissues*
- *scissors*
- *ruler*
- *paper punch*

The foundations that support buildings, bridges, and towers must be able to resist the forces of compression. The decks of suspension bridges or the roofs of some buildings are suspended from cables. Here the forces are tension forces. To be certain that these cables can support the necessary weight, architects must know the tensile strength of the materials used to make the cables.

In this activity you will measure the compression and tensile strength of paper. To measure its compression strength, roll a sheet of paper into a hollow column and tape it together as shown in Figure 10a. Stand it on a spring-type bathroom scale and push straight down on the tube with a book as shown. Be careful to push it straight down. How much force is needed to crush the tube?

The Golden Gate Bridge in San Francisco is one of the largest
suspension bridges in the world. It has a total length of 2,737
meters (8,981 feet).

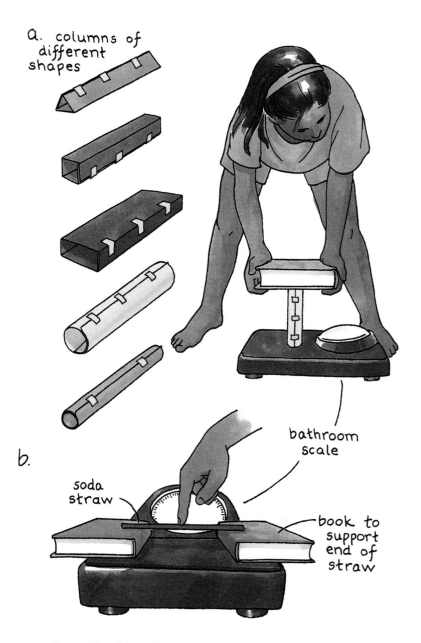

a. columns of different shapes

b.

soda straw

bathroom scale

book to support end of straw

Figure 10: a. Measuring the lengthways compression strength of a paper tube. b. Measuring the sideways compression strength of a soda straw.

Try testing some different paper tubes. Use two sheets of paper to make a tube. Does the thickness of the tube affect its strength? Does doubling the thickness double the compression strength? Being careful to keep the wall thickness the same, does the diameter of the tube affect the compression strength?

Does the shape of the tube affect its strength? To find out, you can crease the paper to make tubes that are square, rectangular, or triangular in cross section as shown.

Measure the compression strength of a paper soda straw using a bathroom scale. Notice how the straw is made. How does it differ from the paper cylinders you made? Compare the compression strength of a paper soda straw and a plastic soda straw. What do you find?

Next, measure the sideways compression strength of a soda straw as shown in Figure 10b. How do the sideways and lengthways compression strengths of a straw compare?

To test the tensile strength of paper, you can use a pail on a loop of paper as shown in Figure 11a. To avoid cutting the paper, suspend the loop from a piece of dowel and wrap a soft pad such as a pot holder around the pail's handle. Place the pail in a sink. Have a friend add water until the weight in the pail breaks the paper.

Use this apparatus to measure the strength of different brands of paper towels. Why should the width and length of the loops of all the different brands of paper towels be the same? Which brand is the strongest? Or are they all about the same? How about other kinds of paper—wrapping, writing, newspaper, facial tissues, etc. Which is the strongest? Does the length of the paper loop affect its tensile strength?

To see how shape affects tensile strength, cut a sheet of 8½ by 11-in. paper into strips that are about 22 cm (8½ in.) long and about 2 cm (¾ in.) wide. Some of the shapes you might try are shown in Figure 11b, but you might like to design some of your own. You can pull on the ends of the strips until they break. If they are too strong for one person to

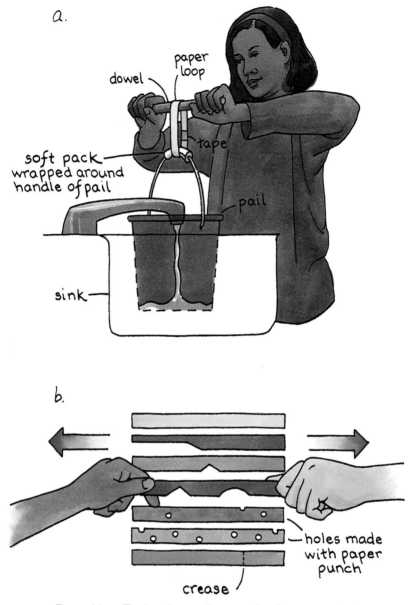

a.

paper loop

dowel

tape

soft pack wrapped around handle of pail

pail

sink

b.

holes made with paper punch

crease

Figure 11: a. Testing the tensile strength of a paper strip. b. Testing the relative tensile strength of different-shaped paper strips.

pull apart, ask someone to pull on one end while you pull on the other. But before you do, mark the point where you think each strip will break. Did all the strips break where you thought they would? Did any surprise you? If they did, try to figure out why they broke where they did.

What is the tensile strength of a paper soda straw? Of a plastic soda straw? How could you test the compression and tensile strength of materials other than paper?

★   **A C T I V I T Y   7**

SIZE, WEIGHT, VOLUME, AND AREA

MATERIALS
■ *modeling clay*
■ *ruler*
■ *balance or scale, 0–500 g (0–16 oz)*

Architects often make three-dimensional models of the buildings they design, but they are well aware that the models are not simply scaled-down versions of the actual buildings. To see why, consider what happens when you double the dimensions of an object.

Use a piece of modeling clay to make a cube 1 in. on each side as shown in Figure 12. This cube has a volume of 1 in.^{3} The total area of its surface is 6 in.^{2} Explain why.

Weigh the cube on a balance. How much does it weigh?

Now make a second cube 2 in. on a side. What is the volume of this cube? What is its total surface area? What has doubling each dimension done to the object's volume? To its total surface area? Compare the volumes and surface areas of the two cubes. What is the ratio of the volume of the second cube to that of the first cube? What is the ratio of their surface areas?

Write the following two sentences on a sheet of paper. (Don't write in this book!) "When the dimensions of an ob-

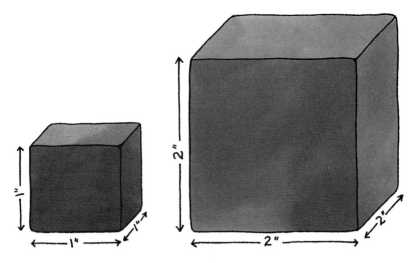

Figure 12. Two cubes, one twice as long, wide, and high as the other, can be made from clay. How will the volumes, surface areas, and weights of the two cubes compare?

ject are doubled, the surface area increases ___ times and the volume increases ___ times. The square of two (2^2) is ___, and the cube of two (2^3) is ___." Fill in the blanks in the sentences you have written with the proper numbers.

Approximately how much do you think the second cube (2 in. on a side) will weigh? Weigh it. Were you right? If you didn't predict its weight correctly, do you see now where you erred in your thinking?

STRENGTH AND AREA

MATERIALS
- *thread*
- *water*

- *sink*
- *plastic pail*
- *small piece of wooden dowel or round pencil*
- *soft pad such as a pot holder*
- *bathroom scale or balance, 0−5 kg (0−11 lb)*

As you can see from Figure 13a, doubling the thickness of a support quadruples its area of cross section. But how is the strength of a material related to its area of cross section? To find out, you can measure the weight needed to break a thread. Tie one end of a thread to the handle of a plastic pail. Hold onto the other end and suspend the pail by the thread over a sink as shown in Figure 13b. Have a friend open the faucet so water runs slowly into the pail. When the thread breaks, the water should be turned off immediately.

Weigh the pail and its contents. How much weight was required to break the single strand of thread?

To double the area of cross section, you can simply suspend the pail from a loop of thread (see Figure 13c) and repeat the experiment. To avoid cutting the thread, suspend the thread from a piece of dowel at the top. Wrap a soft pad such as a pot holder around the pail's handle. How much weight do you predict will be required to break the thread this time? Was your prediction approximately right?

Building and Weight on Earth and in Space

As you have seen, doubling the dimensions of an object increases its weight by eight times and its surface area by four times. The strength of timbers, stones, steel, or whatever is used to support weight doubles when the area of cross section doubles and quadruples when the diameter doubles. If an architect wants to double the size of a building, he or she must more than double the cross sec-

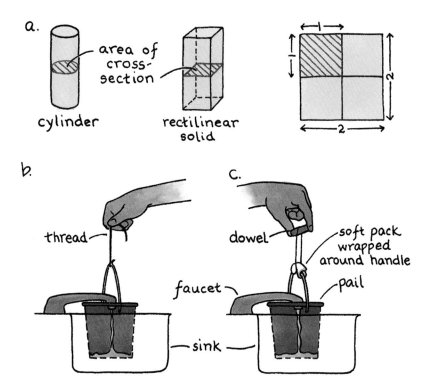

Figure 13: a. The area of cross section of a cylinder and a rectilinear solid. As you can see, doubling the width (or diameter) quadruples the area. b. Measuring the breaking strength of thread. c. Measuring the breaking strength of thread with twice as much cross sectional area.

tion of the supporting materials or use stronger materials. For example, a steel frame might be used instead of wood.

For objects constructed in space, such as space stations orbiting the earth, architects do not have to worry about weight. Why? What would be different for architects planning buildings to be constructed on the moon?

3

ARCHITECTURE, MATHEMATICS, AND BEAUTY

Many believe that harmony in architecture, like harmony in music, can be explained through mathematics. The idea that mathematics and beauty are related stems from Pythagoras, a Greek philosopher who lived in the sixth century B.C. He and his followers (the Pythagoreans) believed that all knowledge arises from numbers. Pythagoras discovered that the sound of a musical note depends on the frequency of vibration of the string or air column that gives rise to the sound. Whether or not two notes played together are harmonious depends on the ratio of their frequencies. (A ratio is one number divided by another, such as ½, ⅔, ⅝, and is indicated as 1:2, for example.) According to Pythagoras, the lower the whole number ratio, the greater the harmony. Later, people who practiced architecture believed they had found the mathematical key to beauty in architecture. They called it the Golden Ratio or the Golden Section. It is the subject of Activity 9.

THE GOLDEN RATIO

MATERIALS
- *paper*
- *sharp pencil*
- *ruler*
- *drawing or carpenter's square (right angle)*
- *drawing compass*
- *calculator (optional)*

It may have been a geometric construction that led to the Golden Ratio. To see how this might have happened, draw a square 10 cm (4 in.) on a side like the one (ABCD) shown in Figure 14. Extend the base line AB to a point near the edge of the paper. Then divide the square into two equal rectangles (AEFD and EBCF). This is done by the dotted line EF in the drawing. Using a compass, draw the arc of a circle whose center is at E and whose radius (EC) is the diagonal of the rectangle EBCF. The arc, shown by dots in the drawing, crosses the extended base AB at G. Use the measurements of BG and BC to construct the rectangle BGHC.

The ratio of AB to BG (AB:BG) is defined as the Golden Ratio. Rectangle BGHC is said to be a Golden Rectangle because the ratio of its long side to its short side is the Golden Ratio. Why is the ratio BC:BG the same as the ratio AB:BG? After making careful measurements, what do you find the Golden Ratio to be?

The actual value of the Golden Ratio is very close to 1.618. It can be approximated by the ratio 8:5.

To see why Greek mathematicians viewed this ratio with awe, consider the ratio of (AB + BG) to AB; that is, (AB + BG):AB. How does it compare with the ratio AB:BG?

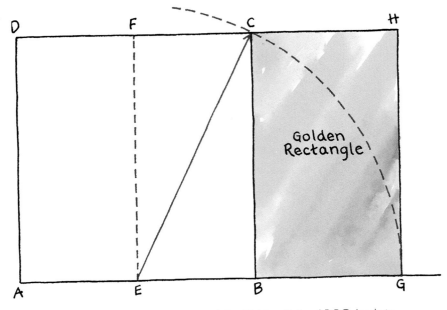

Figure 14. Construction of the Golden Ratio, AB:BG, leads to the Golden Rectangle, BGHC.

As you have probably found, the extended length—BG—added to the original length—AB—bears the same ratio to the original length—AB—as did the original length—AB—to the extended length—BG. That is,

$$\frac{(AB + BG)}{AB} = \frac{AB}{BG.}$$

In real numbers, if AB = 1.618 and BG = 1, we see that:

$$\frac{(1.618 + 1)}{1.618} = 1.618.$$

Can you find any other numbers for which this holds true?

Consider, too, a series of numbers such that each number is the sum of the two preceding ones, such as:

1, 1, 2, 3, 5, 8, 13, 21, 34, 55 . . .

Can you find a single number, call it *n,* that follows the same rule when raised to increasing powers; namely, each term is the sum of the two preceding terms? The number 1 doesn't work (see the series below):

$$1^0, 1^1, 1^2, 1^3, 1^4, 1^5, \ldots$$

It doesn't work because 1 raised to any power is 1. For example, 1^2 (1 x 1) is the same as 1^3 (1 x 1 x 1). Both equal 1 because 1 x 1 = 1 and 1 x 1 x 1 = 1. Therefore, 1^2, which is 1, does not equal $1^0 + 1^1$, which is 1 + 1 = 2. (Any number raised to the 0 power is 1.)

Does the number 2 work? In the series below does each term equal the sum of the two terms that precede it?

$$2^0, 2^1, 2^2, 2^3, 2^4, 2^5 \ldots$$

Can you find any number that works?

There is one such number! Try the Golden Ratio shown below. You'll find a calculator very helpful!

$$(1.618)^0, (1.618)^1, (1.618)^2, (1.618)^3, (1.618)^4, (1.618)^5 \ldots$$

If you construct a square inside a Golden Rectangle (BGHC in Figure 14) using the short side of the rectangle, the remaining rectangle, shown as IJHC in Figure 15, will be a Golden Rectangle. This process of producing smaller Golden Rectangles inside larger ones can go on indefinitely. And the reverse is also true, larger Golden Rectangles can be constructed in a never ending process starting from a small one.

Many architects and artists believe the Golden Rectangle provides harmony in buildings. Figure 16 shows the Parthenon with its roof reconstructed. Notice how nicely it fits the outline of a Golden Rectangle.

Look for Golden Rectangles in pictures of buildings and in buildings themselves. How many can you find? Do you think such buildings are more attractive than buildings that do not fit inside Golden Rectangles?

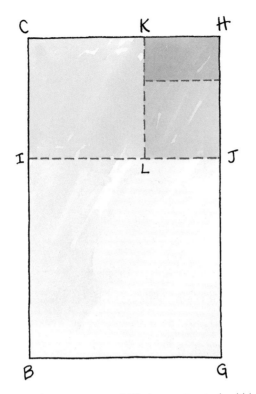

C K H

I L J

B G

Figure 15. When a square, BGJI, is constructed within the Golden Rectangle BGHC, a new Golden Rectangle, IJHC, is formed. This new rectangle can be divided to form still another Golden Rectangle, LJHK, and so on indefinitely.

Can you find Golden Rectangles in other places? How about picture frames? Books? Furniture? Which is closer to being a Golden Rectangle, legal (8.5 by 14-in.) or regular (8.5 by 11-in.) size paper?

Architecture, Beauty, and Order

The idea that beauty in architecture is inherently associated with the ratio of numbers was not limited to the Greeks. Vitruvius, a first century B.C. Roman architect, revived the classical architecture of Greece. In designing buildings he established rules governing

43

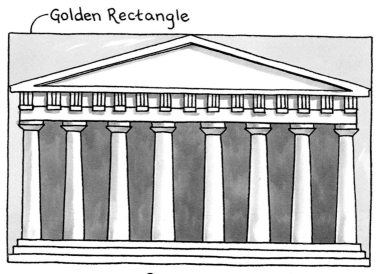

Golden Rectangle

Parthenon

Figure 16. Notice how the Parthenon fits the outline of a Golden Rectangle.

the diameter, height, and spacing of the columns used to support beams. In buildings where the columns were very close together, he said the columns should be separated by a distance equal to ½ the diameter of the columns. The height of such columns should be 10 times the diameter of the columns. In buildings that did not have to support massive beams, the columns could be farther apart. Here, he argued, the columns should be separated by 4 column diameters and rise to a height 8 times the diameter of the column.

His emphasis, as you can see, is not the size of the column but the ratio of the diameter of the columns to their height and separation. Only these ratios, he believed, provided an architecture that would be pleasing to view.

Andrea Palladio, a sixteenth-century Italian architect, believed there were seven ideal plans for a room—a circle, a square, and five rectangles with very definite ratios for length and width (see Figure 17a). He also described a method for determining ideal ceiling heights based on arithmetic and geometric progressions.

Le Corbusier, a twentieth-century architect whose real name was Charles Edouard Jeanneret (1887–1965), saw the Golden Ratio as a reflection of the mathematics of the human body. Thus, the use of the Golden Ratio in architecture expresses the beauty inherent in the human form. The numbers found in Figure 17b are rounded off to the nearest centimeter. They show the proportions of a person 183 cm (6 ft) tall. How many approximate Golden Ratios can you find among these numbers?

Symmetry, Hierarchy, and Other Things Architects Think About

Most architects think that symmetry or balance in a building is important and related to beauty. The two most common forms of symmetry are bilateral symmetry and radial symmetry. The human body, as shown in Figure 18a, has bilateral symmetry; that is, the right side of your body is like the left side. You have a right hand and a left hand, a right eye and a left eye, a right ear and a left ear. The right side of your body is pretty much a mirror image of the left side.

Bilateral symmetry can be found in many buildings. A dormitory with a central corridor onto which many rooms open, a central bathroom between two bedrooms, or a gymnasium with bleachers on either side and a basketball court in between are all examples of bilateral symmetry.

In radial symmetry, there is a balance of elements about two or more axes that intersect at a central point as shown in Figure 18b. A starfish has radial symmetry. Many architects find radial symmetry particularly beautiful and appealing. Where have you seen a building or a landscape with radial symmetry?

Architects often use size, shape, or location to provide hierarchy; that is, to distinguish some aspect of a building or a site as

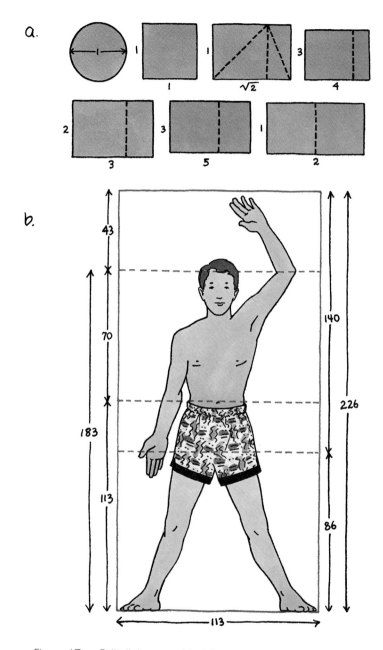

Figure 17: a. Palladio's seven ideal floor plans. Beauty was to be found in the ratio of dimensions, not in size. b. Le Corbusier's use of the human body to arrive at the Golden Ratio. Measurements are in centimeters.

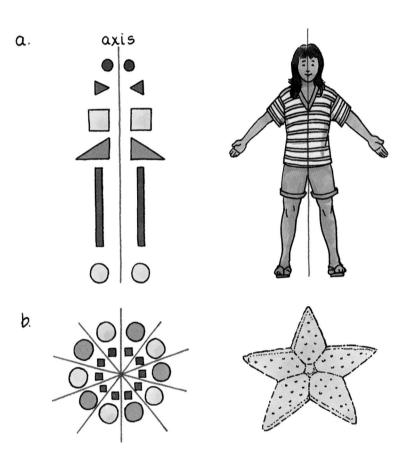

a.   axis

b.

Figure 18: a. Bilateral symmetry: similar elements on either side of a single axis. b. Radial symmetry: similar elements about two or more axes that intersect at a point—a starfish, for example.

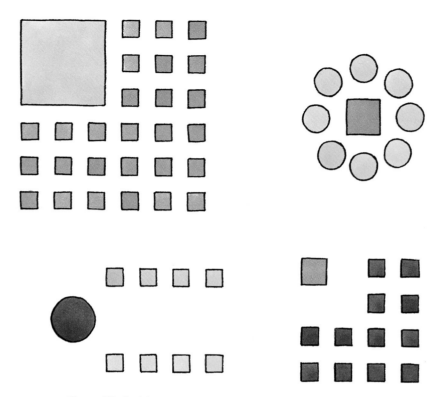

Figure 19. Architects use size, shape, and location to emphasize some aspect of a building or site. How is hierarchy achieved in each of the plans shown?

more important or significant than the rest. Figure 19 shows several ways in which this can be done. What examples of hierarchy can you find in buildings?

A large number of architects, like the artists who design wallpaper, find beauty in repetition. The repetition may be of shape, size, or various details. Some architects prefer linear sequences—repetition along a line or axis; others like to use a radial sequence—repetition along the radii of circles; still others prefer random repetition that requires the viewer to search for repetition. What examples of repetition can you find in architecture?

Some architects emphasize vertical lines as seen in the CBS Building in New York City. Others emphasize horizontal lines.

This is evident in the Robie house designed by Frank Lloyd Wright (1869–1959). The Lab Tower at the Johnson Wax Building in Racine, Wisconsin, reveals that Wright also liked to "soften" the corners of buildings. He seemed to feel that sharp corners were less appealing than round corners.

The Robie House in Chicago was designed by Frank Lloyd Wright to look like a series of horizontal layers floating above the ground.

4

TOWARD THE SKY: TWENTIETH-CENTURY ARCHITECTURE

Several technological developments provided a base for the dramatic changes in architecture that appeared in the twentieth century. Although concrete had been used by Roman builders, new ways of strengthening it improved and expanded its use in construction. Strong concrete and the invention of the elevator by Elisha Otis (1811–1861) in 1854 led architects to design ever taller buildings. However, taller buildings required thicker walls and foundations—factors that increased building costs.

The development of the Bessemer process, which converted iron to steel by mixing melted iron with carbon and various metals, gave architects a new and extremely strong framework for building. Steel frames, in turn, led to new methods of construction that allowed buildings to rise to unprecedented heights. Soaring buildings let landowners make the greatest use of city land where prices, too, were soaring.

The gasoline engine provided a new way to power cement and concrete mixers, pile drivers, hoists, bulldozers, and cranes, which meant construction became faster and required less labor. At the same time, construction became speedier through the use of steel scaffolding and prefabricated materials.

Skyscrapers were preceded by another less dramatic invention—a method of manufacturing nails. With nails, architects soon realized they could build what came to be called balloon frames. Balloon frames are still the most popular form of construction in residential homes.

Balloon Frame Houses

Inexpensive manufactured nails made it possible to frame buildings with 2 by 4s rather than heavy beams. Balloon framing, which eliminated the need for dovetail or mortise and tenon joints, revolutionized the building industry.

In a sense balloon framing was the forerunner of the steel framing used in skyscrapers. In both, a relatively open frame encloses space, and, in both, nonsupporting walls are hung on the frame.

✖ ACTIVITY 10

NAILS AND BALLOON FRAMING

MATERIALS
- *nails, 12 d penny (3¼ in.)*
- *hammer*
- *2 by 4s*
- *saw*
- *glue*

Ask an adult to help you use nails and a hammer to join 2 by 4s as shown in Figure 20a. Then use a saw and glue to join two other 2 by 4s using a mortise and tenon joint as shown in Figure 20b. Why do you think balloon framing became so popular after nails became common and inexpensive?

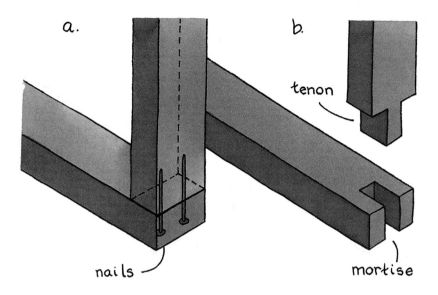

a.

b.

tenon

nails

mortise

Figure 20: a. Joining 2 by 4s with nails. b. Joining 2 by 4s with a mortise and tenon joint.

Building in Concrete

Roman builders made concrete by mixing pozzolana (volcanic ash), slaked lime, sand, and aggregate (stones). They discovered the mixture would harden even under water, which made it very useful in building bridges and aqueducts. A similar concrete was rediscovered by Joseph Aspdin (1799–1855), an English builder, in 1824. He called it portland cement, hoping that it would be used in place of the popular limestone from Portland, England. Portland cement is made by heating in a kiln a mixture of limestone and clay rich in oxides of calcium, aluminum, iron, and silicon. After cooling, the material is ground to a fine powder and mixed with small amounts of gypsum. The particles in the resulting fine gray powder we call cement are less than $\frac{1}{200}$ inch in diameter.

To make concrete, the cement is mixed with water, sand, and crushed stones. The mix is poured into forms where it slowly hardens—a process that goes on for years. Although concrete can resist compression, it has the same defect as stone—it breaks easily when bent.

In 1867 Joseph Monier (1823–1906) obtained a patent for reinforced concrete, which consists of iron rods embedded in the concrete. Iron, which has good tensile strength, provided a concrete that could withstand tension. About a quarter of a century later, Francois Hennibeque (1842–1921) used iron hoops as well as rods in developing a concrete that resisted shear as well as tension.

To make strong wheels, wheelwrights used to fit a hot iron tire to the rim of a wooden wheel as tightly as possible. Then they would pour cold water on the iron to cool it rapidly. As the iron tire cooled, it contracted, putting it under permanent tension as it gripped the wheel. In 1928, Eugène Freyssinet (1879–1962) used a similar approach in making prestressed concrete. Steel rods were kept under tension as concrete was poured around them. After the concrete had hardened, the ends of the rods were cut off, leaving the enclosed rods in a state of permanent stress. Prestressed concrete was so much stronger than ordinary concrete in resisting tension and shear that it allowed architects to build much lighter and more beautiful structures.

The availability of reinforced concrete, together with steel and glass, gave architects new freedom in designing buildings. The TWA terminal at Kennedy Airport in New York City is a good example of how reinforced concrete can be used to produce unique architecture. The Hancock Tower is an example of how one architect made extensive use of glass.

The Hancock Tower in Boston, Massachusetts

BUILDING WITH CONCRETE AND MORTAR

MATERIALS

- *boards such as 2 by 4s and 1 by 6s*
- *ready-to-mix concrete or cement, clean sand, and crushed stone*
- *mortar box, wheelbarrow, or pail*
- *trowel*
- *hoe*
- *shovel*
- *water*
- *burlap bags or old towels*
- *hydrated lime*
- *carpenter's level*
- *bricks or stones*

To see how concrete can be used in building, ask an adult to help you build an outdoor concrete structure such as a step or a small wall. Since fresh concrete has a loose structure, you will need to build a form, level across the top, into which you can pour the concrete. The form can be made from boards, but be sure it is well braced because concrete is heavy and will tend to push the forms apart.

To prepare the concrete, you will need a bag of cement, some clean sand, and some crushed stone. (Or you may prefer to buy ready-to-mix concrete in which the dry ingredients have already been mixed in proper proportions.) You can mix the materials in a mortar box, a wheelbarrow, or a pail (if you use small quantities). Add one part cement to two parts sand and mix them together with a hoe or a trowel until the color is the same throughout. Then add three parts stone and mix until uniform. Make a depression in the middle of the pile, pour in some water, and mix some more. Add more water as needed until you have a uniform mixture that is wet throughout. Avoid adding so much water that the mixture becomes soupy. Excess water will result in weak concrete.

Pour or shovel the concrete you have prepared into the form you made. If necessary, mix a second batch to fill the form. A long board can be moved back and forth across the top of the form to make the top surface of the concrete level. Be sure to wash any damp concrete from the tools you used and the vessel in which you mixed the concrete.

Put damp burlap bags or old towels across the concrete to keep it damp for several hours. After a day, you will find that the concrete is quite hard.

To see how mortar can be used to make a brick wall or step, you will need to mix one part cement with one part hydrated lime and six parts sand. (Again, you can buy ready-to-mix mortar.) Add water as you did in making concrete. The final mixture should look like a smooth plastic; it should be soft but not runny.

Place a wet brick or stone in a level position and use a trowel to cover its top with about an inch of mortar. Place a second wet stone or brick on the first one, tap it with the trowel, and use a carpenter's level to be sure it is horizontal. Leave the bricks or stones overnight. You will find that the mortar has bound them firmly together.

To prepare a more substantial concrete or brick structure, it is important that you have a firm foundation built on concrete footings that are below the frost line (the depth to which soil freezes in the winter). To see why, try the next activity.

A C T I V I T Y   1 2

WHY FOOTINGS MUST BE BELOW THE FROST LINE

MATERIALS
- *tall plastic vial with press-in cap*
- *water*
- *freezer*

Find a tall plastic vial that has a press-in cap. Fill the vial with water and press in the cap so that the vial is completely filled with water. A small air bubble will not matter. Place the vial in a freezer and leave it for several hours. After the water has frozen, notice that the cap is no longer in the vial. What happened? What would happen if water froze beneath the foundation of a building. Why is it important that footings for a foundation are below the frost line?

Building Skyward

The Eiffel Tower, built in 1889, was the last soaring structure built of iron. Thereafter, steel became the predominant building material in the construction of factories and skyscrapers, which became increasingly numerous in cities around the world. Perhaps the best known is the 102-story Empire State Building, once the tallest building in the world. The Sears Tower in Chicago is now the world's tallest building at 443 m (1,454 ft). Skyscrapers, which require firm concrete foundations that extend to bedrock, fostered new construction techniques and new opportunities for steeplejacks. The exterior walls of skyscrapers, unlike those of conventional buildings, support no weight. The steel frame provides the building's strength and basic structure. Walls, referred to as the building's skin, are bolted to spandrels—horizontal steel beams secured to the upright frame. The prefabricated walls are positioned after the frame is built. The floors (and ceilings) are concrete slabs reinforced with metal and wire mesh that lie on steel girders linking the upright I beams.

★   **A C T I V I T Y 1 3**

BUILDING TOWERS OF CLAY

MATERIALS
- *one pound of modeling clay*
- *refrigerator*

Although clay readily succumbs to forces of compression, tension, and shear, it is much less expensive than steel. Cost, not strength, led to the selection of clay as a building material for this activity.

What is the tallest tower you can build from one pound of modeling clay? You might like to look at a variety of towers before you start. Should the tower be a cylinder, a cone, a rectangular solid, or some other shape?

Can you make a tower taller if you make its inside hollow? Can you make a taller tower if you build it on its side using soft clay and then place it in the refrigerator until the clay hardens?

An office building under construction in Pennsylvania

You will find, as do architects, that the best way to plan a tower is to start at the top and work your way down. Find how much clay is needed to support the part above it. An architect will make sure a tall building is safe by making each part stronger than necessary to support the weight above it. However, if the building is made too strong, money is wasted and another architect's plan will be chosen.

★ **ACTIVITY 14**

PAPER SODA STRAW TOWERS

MATERIALS
■ *paper soda straws*
■ *clay*
■ *straight pins*
■ *masking tape*
■ *rubber bands*

Having measured the compression strength of hollow paper tubes in Activity 6, you know that a soda straw has very good lengthwise compression strength for its weight. To see how the compression strength of a cylindrical tube compares with a long square-shaped tube, make four creases lengthwise along a straw to give it a square cross section. Then test the compression strength of this straw with a regular one. How do the compression strengths of straws with circular and square cross sections compare?

A single, upright straw stuck in a clay base is in itself a tower. However, you can join straws together by inserting one into the end of another or by joining them with pins as shown in Figure 21a. If you use pins, cover the sharp points with masking tape as shown. How tall a tower can you make by joining one straw to another? How tall can you make the tower if you fasten several straws together to make a base and gradually taper the number as you go higher (see Figure 21b)?

★ **ACTIVITY 15**

SODA STRAWS, TRIANGLES, AND TOWERS

MATERIALS
- *straight pins*
- *paper or plastic soda straws*
- *rulers*
- *scissors*
- *masking tape*
- *clay*
- *thread*

In towers, and in architecture generally, the triangle is a very important shape. To see why, use pins to fasten four straws into a square as shown in Figure 22a. Use strips of masking tape to cover the ends of the pins so you will not get scratched

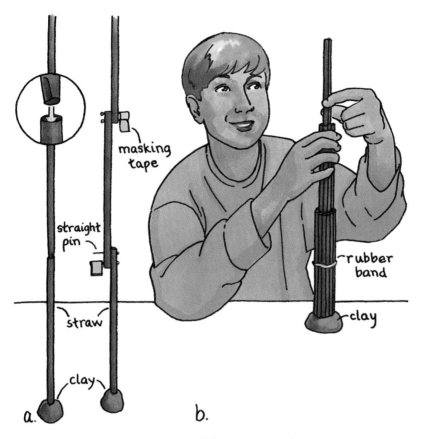

Figure 21: a. Two ways to join straws to make a tower.
b. A tapered tower using "bundles" of straws.

(see Figure 22b). Notice how easy it is to change the shape of the square.

Now place another straw diagonally across the square to divide it into two triangles as shown in Figure 22c. How has the addition of this diagonally placed straw changed the rigidity of the structure? Why do you think triangles are so important in architecture and construction?

Make a tetrahedron using pins and soda straws as shown in Figure 22d. Why do you think this structure is so strong?

What is the tallest tower you can build from straws using

diagonal cross members like the one in Figure 22c? Why is it more practical and economical to build a tower this way rather than packing decreasing numbers of straws together as the tower ascends the way you did in the previous activity?

If you look closely at the tall, skinny antennas used to broadcast television and radio waves, you will see that they are supported by strong cables or wires, called guys. Usually three guys are fastened at any given height on the tower. The total number of guys depends on the height of the tower.

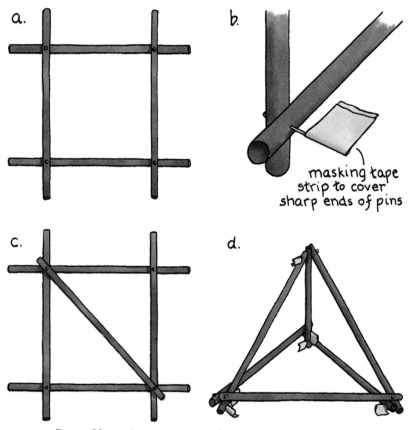

Figure 22: a. A square made from soda straws and pins. b. Cover the ends of the pins with strips of masking tape. c. The same square divided into triangles by means of a fifth straw pinned as a diagonal. d. A tetrahedron has four triangular faces.

A tall straw tower can also be built using guys. You can use thread for guys. The guys can be fastened to the floor with clay as shown in Figure 23. Why are two guys at a given height not enough? Why is it not necessary to have four guys—one for each direction? How tall can you make a straw tower using guys?

Hurricanes or freezing rain and wind can cause guyed towers to topple. How much wind can your guyed tower sustain? You can use a multiple-speed fan and a wind gauge to test your tower's resistance to wind.

Why is a flashing light attached to the top of most radio and television antennas?

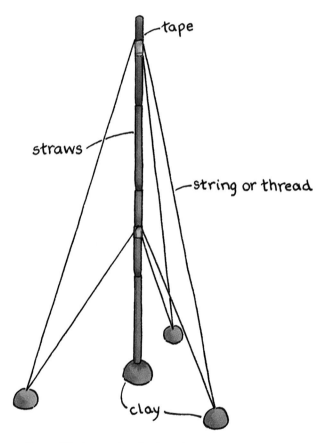

Figure 23. A guyed soda straw tower.

The earliest bridge was probably a log placed across a stream so it could be crossed without getting wet feet. Such a bridge is a beam span like the one you tested in Activity 5. It is one of the three structural types of bridge spans—beam, arch, and suspension.

A beam span bridge may simply be a pair of beams with floor-boards to support traffic. In all beam bridges the ends of the beams, resting on earth, exert a downward force. Longer beam bridges may consist of several beams placed end to end resting on piers spaced across the opening.

Truss beam bridges consist of an upper and lower chord (beam) with web members that connect the two chords. There are many types of truss bridges. One of them is shown in Figure 24a. Panel points where the various parts intersect are joined by nuts and bolts, rivets, or welds. Loads in truss bridges bear on the intersections, producing tension and compression and preventing bending. Trusses are also used by architects in designing roofs.

As you saw in Activity 15, a triangular structure, which is the basic design for the truss beam bridges, is a particularly sturdy form. This is because a triangle is the only figure that cannot change shape without changing the length of its sides. Consequently, if strong material is firmly fastened at the angles of the triangular frame, the frame will not be deformed by its own weight or by external forces such as wind.

A cantilevered bridge (see Figure 24b) is like two diving boards that meet in the middle to span a pool. The free ends of the two beams, with counterweights to keep their on-ground ends in place, can be connected directly or by a short beam. Although a corbel arch bridge (see Figure 24c) resembles an arch, it is really a series of cantilevers, one atop the other, that span an opening.

Unlike beam bridges, which all push downward against the earth, arch bridges exert a force outward as well as downward. Roman architects and builders, who were partial to the semicircular arch, realized that it was necessary to provide strong buttresses at the

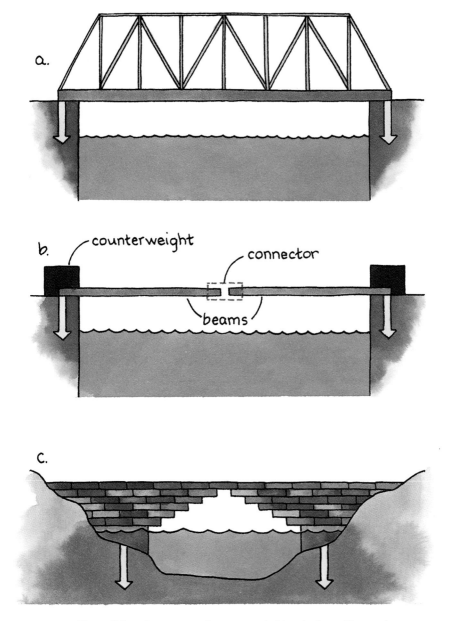

Figure 24: a. A truss-type beam span bridge. b. A cantilevered bridge. c. A corbel arch bridge is really a cantilevered bridge.

sides of the arch to prevent them from collapsing. The same was true of medieval cathedral architects who designed flying buttresses to support the huge arched vaults. Today, reinforced concrete and steel arch span bridges can be found throughout the world.

The simplest suspension bridge is the "bridge" used by tightrope walkers. The first practical suspension bridges were foot bridges made of vines or braided roots, but first-century Chinese used iron chains to build a 76-m- (250-ft-) long suspension bridge across the Lantshang River.

Unlike arch bridges, which thrust outward, suspension bridges pull their tall anchoring supports inward. Of course, where there are several spans in series, the intermediate points of suspension are pulled in both directions. For long spans, suspension bridges are less expensive to build, but, because of the uniqueness of locations, every bridge requires a design that matches the terrain it must traverse.

Roads

To connect the regions of an expanding empire, Roman architects designed and supervised the construction of more than 80,000 km (50,000 mi) of roads. The roads facilitated trade and the movement of soldiers. Their roads varied in width from 5 to 10 m (16–33 ft), depending on location and traffic, but they were well built with a deep and firm base more than 90 cm (3 ft) deep. The layered base, from bottom to top, consisted of layers of rubble, crushed stone, sand, and stone slabs.

After Roman roads fell into disrepair during the fourth century, no satisfactory replacements were built until the 1700s. And it was not until the next century that John Loudon McAdam (1756–1836) in Great Britain rediscovered what was needed to provide good roads. McAdam realized that a long-lasting road required a firm, well-drained, compact base and a cambered surface (to carry off water) so compacted that it was waterproof. Such roads were rare

Winchester Cathedral in England was designed with flying buttresses for support.

in the United States even after the invention of the automobile. McAdam developed the paving we know as macadam, which is widely used in today's roads.

To meet the demands of heavy, high speed trucks and cars developed during the twentieth century, road surfaces were covered with tar or asphalt coated with small stones. Such a surface provided waterproofing and prevented dust in dry weather; the small stones reduced skidding. It was not until the 1930s that reinforced concrete was used as a road surface. In Germany, a new type of road surface—stone-mastic asphalt—has been developed and is now being tested in the United States. It consists of crushed stones held together by a hard asphalt binder that contains fibers or polymer additives. The material resists the rutting that occurs when heavy trucks roll along today's asphalt pavements. This and other materials currently being investigated may provide better and longer-lasting roads.

BRIDGES

MATERIALS

- *two rulers*
- *two thick books*
- *weights such as heavy washers or standard laboratory weights*
- *books of similar thickness*
- *file card (3 by 5 in., 5 by 7 in., or 8 by 10 in.)*
- *masking tape*
- *thread*
- *two sticks*
- *clay*
- *string*
- *paper or plastic soda straws*
- *steel washers*

You built a simple wood beam span bridge in Activity 5 and found that the amount it bends under a load depends on its length, thickness, and the size of the load. If you substituted steel for wood, your beam would be much stronger, of course.

Using two rulers, build a cantilever span across the space between two thick books. Other books placed on the ends of the rulers can serve as counterweights. Test the bending of the spans by placing weights at various points on the rulers. What are some of the problems involved in building a cantilever bridge? How could they be solved?

Build a model of a corbel arch bridge by piling books on top of one another. What problems must be overcome in building a corbel arch bridge?

To see the principle and comparative strength of a simple arch bridge, place a file card across two books that are separated by about two-thirds the length of the card as shown in

Figure 25a. To get a sense of the compression strength of this simple beam span, press downward with your finger at the center of the span. Now use the same card to make an arch span (see Figure 25b) between the two books. Again, press downward at the top of the arch. How does the compression strength of the arch span compare with that of the beam span?

Notice what happens as you press downward on the arch. How can you tell that there is an outward force on the arch? You can see the same thing by using your fingers to convert the flat card into an arch. Which way do you have to push the edges of the card? Which way do the edges of the card push on your fingers?

To see the direction of the tension forces in a suspension bridge, use masking tape to attach several equally spaced steel washers to a piece of thread as shown in Figure 25c. Tape the ends of the thread to the tops of two sticks stuck in clay. Which way does your suspension bridge pull the sticks? What can you do to keep the bridge from collapsing? What is the shape of the thread between the washers?

Ask a friend to hold one end of your suspension bridge while you hold the other. Which way does the thread pull on your fingers? What happens to the tension as you try to make the thread straighter?

Build a suspension bridge using string and soda straws. How much weight will your bridge hold? You might hold a contest to see who can build the strongest 30-cm- (1-ft-) long, 8-cm- (3 in.-) wide suspension bridge from 100 straws and 3 m (10 ft) of string.

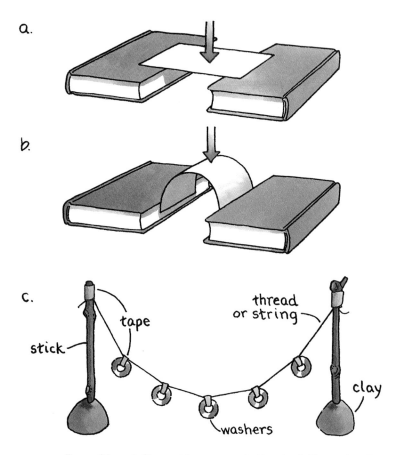

Figure 25: a. A file-card beam span bridge. b. A file-card arch span bridge. c. A thread suspension span bridge.

BUILDING AN ARCH

MATERIALS
- *Styrofoam square 3 feet on a side and 2 inches thick*
- *pencil*
- *string*
- *ruler*
- *large protractor*
- *serrated knife*
- *masking tape*
- *books*

A casual observer might wonder why an arch doesn't fall. But if you look carefully, or better, if you build an arch, you will see that gravity pulls the stones against one another. As long as the end (springer) stones are firmly anchored, the arch will hold itself together. To build a small arch, find a square piece of Styrofoam that is 3 feet on a side and 2 inches thick. Use a pencil and a string as a compass and draw two semicircles centered on one side of the square (see Figure 26). The larger semicircle with a radius of 18 in. will reach across one side of the square. Draw the second semicircle with a radius of 14 in. so that the distance between the two semicircles is 4 in. Next, use a large protractor to mark out radii approximately 14° apart (ideally 13.8°).

Ask an adult to help you cut out the arch and the 13 individual "stones" with a serrated knife. Notice that the keystone and the springers have slightly different shapes than the more common voussoirs (wedge-shaped pieces that form an arch).

Use a little masking tape to hold the stones in place and anchor the springers by using books as buttresses. Your arch should stand by itself as long as the wind does not blow it over.

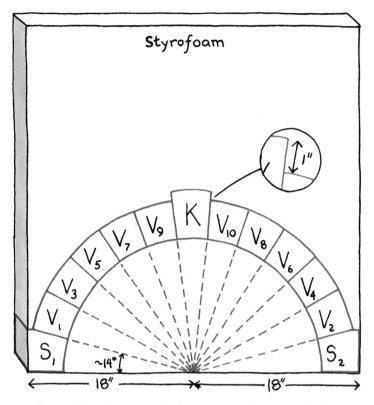

Figure 26. A Roman arch: the top central stone is the key-stone, K. The two stones at either end, S_1 and S_2, are the springers. The remaining 10 stones are the voussoirs, V_1–V_{10}.

See if you can build an arch with more or less curvature than the Roman (semicircular) arch.

So-called barrel arches, shaped like the inside of half a cylinder, were constructed by building a series of arches one after the other. The Romans also erected the first domed buildings, which are hemispherical arches. How did they do this?

See if you can build an arch span bridge.

A TRUSS BRIDGE

MATERIALS

- *straight pins*
- *masking tape*
- *paper soda straws*
- *ruler*
- *two books or a table*
- *scissors*
- *weights such as washers or standard laboratory weights*
- *cardboard strips*
- *paper fasteners*
- *wood glue*

Use straight pins, tape, and soda straws, some of them cut in half, to build a truss bridge that spans the gap between two books or a table. To avoid being scratched, place strips of masking tape over the ends of the pins. One side of such a bridge is shown in Figure 27. How would you fasten two such sides together? What could you use as flooring for your bridge? Cardboard is one possibility. Would corrugated cardboard be stronger than flat cardboard? If you find the corrugated cardboard to be stronger, can you explain why it is stronger?

Once your bridge is built, test it to see how much weight it can hold. Your bridge's strength may surprise you.

Build another truss bridge using cardboard strips and paper fasteners. You might hold a contest to see who can build the strongest 30-cm- (1-ft-) long, 8-cm- (3-in.-) wide truss bridge from one sheet of cardboard and 50 paper fasteners. The winner can be determined by placing a bridge across two thick books and adding more and more weight to the center of the bridge until it collapses.

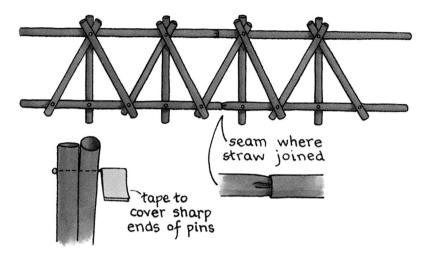

Figure 27. One side of a truss bridge built from soda straws and pins.

Antidisaster Architecture

Buildings subject to hurricanes and earthquakes require special construction. Far too often, the necessary building precautions are ignored and the result is disastrous.

To avoid hurricane damage, homes should not be built close to the ocean where high-velocity winds and/or extraordinary tides that accompany hurricanes can reduce buildings to scattered splinters or floating boards. Those who cannot resist the desire to build by the sea should at least seek the services of an architect skilled in the design of hurricane-resistant buildings. Such an architect will recommend that

1. Houses built near a beach should be constructed on elevated pilings that raise the building above the highest tides ever measured at the site. The pilings will be driven deeply into the soil so that erosion cannot wash the structure into the ocean.

2. The house, if erected on soil well above maximum high tide level, might be built of reinforced concrete to resist high winds.

3. Roofs should be steeply pitched. Hurricane winds tend to lift

flat or low pitched roofs. Steeply pitched roofs, on the other hand, are actually pushed downward by high winds.

4. Roofs, walls, and foundations should be lashed together with bolts and steel straps. This will reduce the likelihood of roofs being blown away or frames moved off their foundations.

5. Storm shutters should be installed. The shutters can be used to cover windows and doors during hurricanes. Strong winds can sometimes blow open doors and break windows. Once winds enter a house, they may create a pressure sufficient to blow out walls or lift the roof.

In the case of buildings constructed in earthquake-prone areas such as California, architects recommend that

1. Buildings should be constructed on firm, not loose, soil.

2. Family-style homes should be made of wooden frames firmly fastened to a reinforced concrete foundation. Materials such as stucco, stone, brick, or unreinforced concrete that are brittle or lack tensile strength should not be used.

3. Multistoried buildings should be built on a steel frame because steel is flexible. Columns, walls, and foundation should be woven together so that the entire structure will move as one piece. No part of the building should be free to move by itself. Fixtures inside the structure, such as cabinets, computers, desks, and so on, should be firmly fixed to walls or floors so they cannot move or fall when the building vibrates.

4. A box-shaped structure is safer than L-shaped buildings because the wings on buildings with complex shapes vibrate at a different frequency than the main part of the structure.

Much is still unknown about earthquakes and how best to reduce the damage they cause, but engineers and architects are using shake tables—hydraulically powered steel platforms—to test various building designs. Models are built on the platform, which is then shaken to simulate an earthquake. In this way, various designs and materials can be tested for their resistance to earthquakes.

One thing is certain: buildings, not trembling earth, are the main source of danger during an earthquake. People are killed when buildings collapse or burn during the quake. Running outside should be avoided because more debris falls from the outside of buildings than from within them. The best thing to do is to crawl under a heavy piece of furniture and stay there until the shaking stops.

5

THE SUN AND BUILDING
FOR THE FUTURE

Before humans learned how to mine coal, natural gas, and oil from the earth, many of them used the sun to warm their dwellings. Today, as the abundance of fossil fuels diminishes and the products of their combustion pollute the atmosphere, many architects are designing buildings that use solar energy as a source of heat and electricity. These architects use the scientific principles associated with thermal energy and a growing solar technology to plan buildings that make use of this free source of energy.

Absorbing Solar Energy

Either active or passive solar heating can be used to warm a building. In passive solar heating, sunlight passing through transparent windows is absorbed by materials inside the building. In active solar heating, sunlight is converted to heat when it is absorbed by water, air, or other fluids in solar panels outside the building. The warm fluid is then circulated through the building's interior where it gives up its heat and then back to the panel to be heated again.

In winter the sun's path across the sky is low; in the summer its path is high. By careful design, architects can build roofs with overhangs that allow light to enter a building during the winter, but not in the summer. Another approach is to embed much of the house under ground so that only the south wall is exposed. Since the temperature of the earth remains quite constant, heating and cooling costs for such a house are greatly reduced.

The following activities will help you to see some of the factors architects must consider in designing solar buildings.

★ **ACTIVITY 19**

COLOR AND THE ABSORPTION OF SOLAR ENERGY

MATERIALS
- *construction paper—black, white, green, red, and blue*
- *paper clips*
- *scissors*
- *several identical thermometers*
- *sheet of cardboard*
- *sunlight*
- *measuring cup*
- *tap water*
- *two identical aluminum pie pans*
- *eyedropper*
- *black ink*

Wrap 5-cm (2-in.) by 13-cm (5-in.) sheets of construction paper of different colors around the bulbs of identical thermometers as shown in Figure 28. Use paper clips to hold the paper in place. Place the wrapped thermometers on a sheet of cardboard in a shady place until they reach a steady, uniform temperature. Then place the cardboard in the sun so that all the sheets receive the same amount of sunlight. Record the temperature under each colored paper at 3-minute intervals for 15 minutes. (Alternatively, you can repeat the experiment

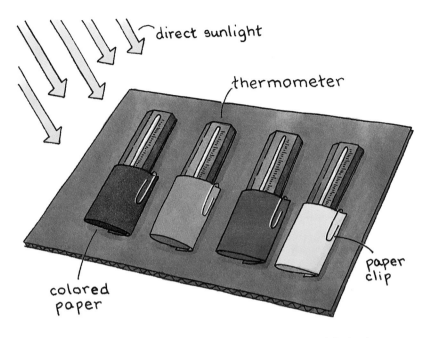

direct sunlight

thermometer

colored
paper

paper
clip

Figure 28. Does color affect the rate at which sunlight is absorbed and changed to heat?

several times with one or two thermometers. The thermometers can be cooled back to air temperature by waving them gently through air.)

Does color have any effect on the rate at which sunlight is converted to heat? If it does, which color seems to be the best light absorber? Which seems to be the best reflector of light?

Place 120 mL (4 oz) of cold tap water in each of two identical aluminum pie pans. Add black ink to one pan to make the water very dark. Add an equal amount of water to the other pan. Place both pans side by side on a sheet of cardboard. Use a thermometer to be sure both pans of water are at the same temperature. Then place them in a warm, sunny place so both receive the same amount of sunlight. Predict in which pan of water the temperature will rise faster. What can you do to test your prediction? Were you right?

Storing Solar Energy

It is not too hard to warm a building with sunlight on a bright sunny day. But if the building is to stay warm at night and on cloudy days, there must be a way to store the heat. Native Americans in the Southwest used thick adobe walls to absorb solar energy during the day. At night these same walls released heat to the space they surrounded. Today, architects and engineers design passive solar heating systems to make use of similar materials that have a capacity for storing large amounts of heat. Large dark-colored drums filled with heat-absorbing matter or thick, dark, concrete walls (Trombe walls) and floors are built in front of south-facing windows to absorb sunlight during the daylight hours. At night these walls release their stored warmth to the air in the building and the windows are covered to reduce heat loss to the cool air outside.

✖ ★   A C T I V I T Y   2 0

HEAT ABSORBERS

MATERIALS
- *identical metal cans (such as empty soup cans)*
- *different kinds of matter such as water, small stones, sand, dirt, and salt*
- *aluminum foil to cover the can that contains water*
- *oven*
- *pot holders*
- *thick sheet of cardboard*
- *thermometer(s), (optional)*
- *flat black paint*

Architects and engineers use good heat absorbers to store the energy in sunlight. You can test some different materials to see

80

which ones might be best for storing heat. Fill several identical metal cans with different kinds of matter. You might use water, small stones, sand, dirt, and salt. Cover the can that contains water to prevent evaporation. Ask an adult to place the cans in a warm 120°F (50°C) oven until all the substances reach oven temperature.

Remove the cans, using pot holders to protect your hands, and place them side by side on a thick sheet of cardboard. You can probably tell by touch which can cools fastest and which slowest, but if possible, measure their temperatures with a thermometer to confirm your touch test. Which of the substances you tested stays warm longest? Which would you recommend for storing solar energy? Based on what you learned in Activity 19, what color would you paint the container in which you store the heat absorber?

Paint each can with flat black paint. Let them dry overnight in the same place, then put them in front of a sunny window or in a sheltered place outdoors where all receive the same amount of sunlight. Which can do you think will warm up fastest? Slowest? After several hours, find the temperature of the material inside each can. Were your predictions correct?

★ **ACTIVITY 21**

DESIGNING ROOF OVERHANG

MATERIALS
- *map or globe*
- *ruler*
- *protractor*

It is easy to find the maximum midday altitude reached by the sun in summer and winter if you know the latitude where you live. You can find your latitude on a map or globe. The sun's highest altitude, which occurs around June 20, is equal to

$$(90° + 23.5°) - \text{(your latitude)}$$

The minimum midday altitude of the sun, which occurs around December 20, is

$$(90° - 23.5°) - \text{(your latitude)}$$

The altitude at the equinoxes (March 20 and September 20) is

$$90° - \text{(your latitude)}$$

With this information, calculate how much roof overhang is needed to shut out the noonday sun from March to September, but allow noonday sun to enter from September to March.

See if you can calculate the origin of the formulas used to determine the midday altitudes of the sun. **Hint:** Remember, the sun is directly over the equator (0° latitude) at the equinoxes. On June 20 it is directly over the latitude 23.5° north of the equator; on December 20 it is directly over the latitude 23.5° south of the equator.

Keeping the Heat Inside

Once a building has been heated, whether by solar energy or other means, architects must design ways to reduce the rate at which heat "leaks" out of the building. This is done by using building materials that are poor conductors of heat and/or by surrounding heated areas with insulation. Insulation is a material such as mineral wool, fiberglass, vermiculite, expanded polyurethane or polystyrene, chopped paper (cellulose), or other materials that have lots of tiny air pockets and transfer heat very slowly.

INSULATION: KEEPING BUILDINGS WARM OR COOL

MATERIALS

- *pitcher*
- *hot tap water*
- *measuring cup or graduated cylinder*
- *tin can, 3 Styrofoam cups*
- *paper cups, large and small*
- *thermometer(s)*
- *clock*
- *pencil and paper*
- *graph paper*

How much does insulation reduce the flow of heat? To find out, fill a pitcher with hot tap water. Pour 120 mL (4 oz) of the hot water into each of four containers—a tin can, a paper cup, a Styrofoam cup, and two Styrofoam cups, one inside the other. Measure and record the initial temperature of the water in each container. Repeat your measurements of the water temperature in each container every five minutes for at least a half hour.

Use the data you have collected to make a graph of temperature versus time as shown in Figure 29. Plot the data for all four containers on the same set of axes. When does the water in each cup cool fastest? Slowest? How does the difference between the temperature of the water and the cooler air around it affect the rate of cooling? Do you need to do a separate experiment to find out?

In which container does the water cool fastest? Slowest? Which container is the best insulator? The poorest insulator?

What do you think will happen to the cooling rate of the best insulated container if you cover it by inverting a similar container over its top? Try it! Were you right?

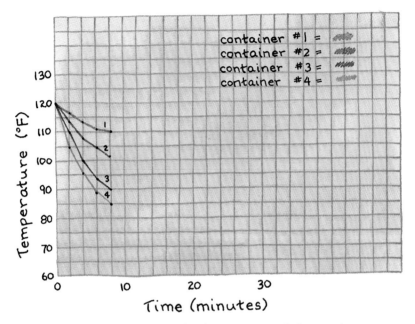

Figure 29. A graph showing how water cools in containers that have different insulation.

Builders warn homeowners not to let their insulation get wet. A leaky roof for example might allow attic insulation to become wet. To compare wet and dry insulation, separate two paper cups, one large and one small, with crumpled pieces of newspaper. Do the same with a second pair of paper cups, but use crumpled paper that has been wet with water. Pour the same amount of hot tap water into the smaller inside cup for both setups and record the initial temperature. Again, measure and record the water temperature in each cup every five minutes for at least a half hour. How do the qualities of wet and dry insulation compare? Are builders right when they warn homeowners not to let their insulation get wet?

Design experiments of your own to find out whether insulation will reduce the rate at which cold things warm as well as the rate at which warm things cool.

GOING FURTHER

- Instructions for building a small house of your own can be found in a book by Les Walker entitled *Housebuilding for Children: Six Different Houses That Children Can Build for Themselves* (The Overlook Press, Woodstock, New York, 1990).
★ • If you'd like to do a project on Native American architecture and build some of their structures, you can find the information you need in a book entitled *American Indian Habitats: How to Make Dwellings and Shelters with Natural Materials,* by Nancy Simon and Evelyn Wolfson (David McKay Company, New York, 1978).
★ • Find out how to build igloos, which are used as temporary shelters by the Aleuts. Then see if you can build an igloo of your own during the winter.
★ • Investigate the various types of architecture, such as Egyptian, classical Greek and Roman, Gothic, Byzantine, Renaissance, Baroque, modern, and so on. Find examples of the various styles and photograph them. Make and exhibit three-dimensional models of each type. What aspects of each style appeal to people? Which is your favorite? Why?
★ • Build a three-dimensional model of a cathedral or the Taj Mahal. A well-illustrated description of how medieval cathe-

drals were built can be found in *Medieval Cathedral* by Fiona Macdonald (Peter Bedrick Books, New York, 1991).

★ • Examine a fireplace. How does it work? Under adult supervision build a model fireplace to show how waste gases are carried up the chimney and not into the house. Investigate how fireplaces might be made more efficient; that is, how more of the heat that goes up the chimney could be transferred to the house.

★ • How tall a tower can you build using dried peas and toothpicks?

★ • What is the tallest tower you can build with a single sheet of paper?

★ • Test various types of wood for bending across a span. Be sure to use pieces that are equal in length, width, and thickness. You might try oak, pine, ash, cedar, and other woods. Which wood would be the best to use for bridge beams?

★ • Wooden boards often contain knots. What effect does a knot have on the strength of wood?

★ • You might enjoy investigating some, or all, of such odd architectural forms as icehouses, lighthouses, gazebos, shanties, firehouses, windmills, covered bridges, and outhouses (also known as backhouses and privys). Which of these forms of architecture still exist? Which have been outmoded by new technology?

★ • Consider the architecture of certain sports equipment. For example, why are there seams on basketballs and baseballs? Why are there dimples on golf balls? What has happened to the shape and design of hockey sticks, baseball bats, lacrosse sticks, and tennis rackets during the past century? Why have these changes taken place?

★ • Based on what you have learned, build a model solar home.

★ • In recent years a number of bridges have failed, often giving rise to loss of life. What are the major causes of bridge failures? What can be done to prevent such failures?

★ • Metals expand in summer's heat and contract in winter's cold.

How do architects take this into account when they design buildings and bridges of steel?

★ • Some animals are great natural architects. You might enjoy investigating, with care, the architectural endeavors of one or more of the following animals: ants (especially carpenter ants), tent caterpillars, wasps, bees, spiders, birds, mice, groundhogs, and, of course, beavers.

★ • Design and build some birdhouses. Are birds more attracted to one design than another? More to one color than another? How must you change your design to accommodate different species?

★ • Twentieth-century architecture reflects the work of such people as Louis Sullivan, Frank Lloyd Wright, Le Corbusier, Ludwig Mies van der Rohe, R. Buckminster Fuller, I. M. Pei, and Richard Rogers. Examine the work of one, several, or all of these architects. What were their contributions to architecture? How are their ideas made evident in their buildings and designs?

GLOSSARY

arch bridge: a bridge made of a curved support that exerts a force outward as well as downward. Strong buttresses must be built at the ends of such a bridge to prevent the arched support from pushing outward and collapsing.

architecture: the designing and construction of buildings.

balloon framing: a method of framing a house with 2 by 4 lumber held together primarily with nails. Such framing eliminated the need for dovetail or mortise and tenon joints and revolutionized the building industry.

beam span bridge: a bridge made from parallel beams with floor boards to support traffic. Both ends of the beams, which rest on earth, exert a downward force. Long beam bridges may consist of several beams placed end to end resting on piers spaced across the opening.

bilateral symmetry: exists when the right side of an object or body is the same as the left side. Your own body is an example of such symmetry.

buttress: a structure used to provide support, usually to a wall or arch. Flying buttresses extend from the walls of a building and prevent those walls from collapsing. The flying buttresses used in building cathedrals often contained an archway through the buttress.

cantilever: a beam, supported at only one end, which projects over a space.

cantilevered bridge: a bridge in which the free ends of two cantilevered beams are connected.

cobwork: a form of construction in which dirt is rammed between parallel boards to form large "bricks," which, after drying, are coated with plaster to repel water.

compression: the forces that squeeze materials together.

concrete: a mixture of cement, water, sand, and stones that hardens to form a strong material.

corbel arch bridge: a bridge resembling an arch, which is really a series of cantilevers, one atop the other.

frequency: the number of happenings per unit time. For example, a certain string on a musical instrument may vibrate 256 times per second.

Golden Ratio: a value very close to 1.618 or approximately 8:5. A rectangle whose length:width ratio is equal to this is called a Golden Rectangle.

hierarchy: in architecture, the principle of constructing a building or a site so that some aspect or part of it will be seen to be more important or significant than other parts.

inclined plane: a simple machine consisting of a surface that slopes from one level to another. Moving a weight to a higher level along the incline requires less force than vertical lifting.

insulation: a material with lots of tiny air pockets that transfers heat very slowly. It is used in buildings to reduce the rate at which heat passes through walls, floors, and ceilings.

lever: a simple machine consisting of a rigid bar that turns on a fixed point (fulcrum) and can be used to change the direction and size of an applied force.

portland cement: a mixture of limestone and clay rich in oxides of calcium, aluminum, iron, and silicon, which is heated in a kiln, cooled, and ground to a fine powder before being mixed with small amounts of gypsum. The particles of the resulting gray powder are less than $\frac{1}{200}$ in. in diameter.

prestressed concrete: a very strong material that has a high resistance to tension and shear. It is made by pouring concrete around steel rods that are under tension.

radial symmetry: a symmetry in which there is a balance of elements about two or more axes that intersect a central point. A starfish is an example of an organism that has radial symmetry.

reinforced concrete: concrete in which iron or steel rods or hoops are embedded to produce a material that has good tensile as well as compression strength.

scale: using a short length to represent a greater length. For example, an architect might draw plans in which one inch on the plan represents one foot of the building actually constructed.

shear: opposing forces that do not act along the same line.

solar energy: the energy available from sunlight.

solar heating (passive): heating accomplished by using materials inside a building to absorb sunlight that is changed to heat upon being absorbed. **(active):** heating accomplished by using water, air, or other fluids in solar panels outside a building to absorb sunlight, which is converted to heat and warms the fluid. The warm fluid is then circulated through the building's interior where it gives up its heat before being returned to the panel to be heated again.

spandrels: horizontal steel beams secured to the upright frame of a skyscraper.

steeplejack: a worker on steeples or other high structures.

stone–mastic asphalt: a mixture of crushed stones held together by a hard asphalt binder that contains fibers or polymer additives.

suspension bridge: a bridge in which the roadway is suspended from cables connected to tall anchoring towers.

tension: forces that tend to pull materials apart.

truss beam bridge: a bridge consisting of an upper and lower chord (beam) with web members that connect the two chords. Loads in truss bridges bear on the intersections in the webbing producing tension and compression that prevent bending.

wheel and axle (windlass): a simple machine consisting of a cylinder and a crank usually with rope attached to the cylinder. Because the radius of the crank is greater than the radius of the cylinder, a force applied to the crank can exert a larger force on a weight fastened to the cylinder, making it easier to lift or pull heavy loads.

UNITS AND THEIR ABBREVIATIONS

LENGTH

English	*Metric*
mile (mi)	kilometer (km)
yard (yd)	meter (m)
foot (ft)	centimeter (cm)
inch (in.)	millimeter (mm)

AREA

English	*Metric*
square mile (mi^2)	square kilometer (km^2)
square yard (yd^2)	square meter (m^2)
square foot (ft^2)	square centimeter (cm^2)
square inch ($in.^2$)	square millimeter (mm^2)

VOLUME

English	*Metric*
cubic mile (mi^3)	cubic kilometer (km^3)
cubic yard (yd^3)	cubic meter (m^3)
cubic foot (ft^3)	cubic centimeter (cm^3)
cubic inch ($in.^3$)	cubic millimeter (mm^3)
ounce (oz)	liter (L)
	milliliter (mL)

MASS

English	*Metric*
pound (lb)	kilogram (kg)
ounce (oz)	gram (g)

TIME

hour (hr)
minute (min)
second (s)

FORCE OR WEIGHT

English	*Metric*
ounce (oz)	newton (N)
pound (lb)	

SPEED OR VELOCITY

English	*Metric*
miles per hour (mi/hr)	kilometers per hour (km/hr)
miles per second (mi/s)	kilometers per second (km/s)
feet per second (ft/s)	meters per second (m/s)
	centimeters per second (cm/s)

TEMPERATURE

English	*Metric*
degrees Fahrenheit (°F)	degrees Celsius (°C)

ENERGY

calorie (cal)
Calorie (Cal)
joule (J)

POWER

watt (W) = joule per second (J/s)

ELECTRICAL UNITS

volt (V)
ampere (A)

MATERIALS

aluminum foil
aluminum pie pans
balance or scale
black ink
boards (various sizes)
books (various sizes)
bricks
burlap bags or old towels
calculator
cardboard sheets
carpenter's level
carpenter's ruler
clay
clock
construction paper (various colors)
crayon (dark color)
drawing compass
drawing or carpenter's square
eyedropper
fan
file card
flat black paint
freezer
glue
graph paper
hammer
heavy washers or standard laboratory
   weights
hoe
hydrated lime
map or globe
masking tape
measuring cup
metal cans

metric ruler
modeling clay
mortar box or wheel barrow
nails
natural materials (small trees,
   branches, leaves, vines, stones,
   soil, etc.)
oven
paper (variety of types)
paper and plastic soda straws
paper clips
paper cups
paper fasteners
paper punch
paper towels (different brands)
pencil sharpener
pencils
pitcher
plastic pail
plastic vial with press-in cap
pot holders
protractor
ready-to-mix concrete
refrigerator
round stick or broom handle
rubber bands
ruler
salt
sand
saw
scissors
serrated knife
shovel
sink

soft pad (such as a pot holder)
soft stick
straight pins
string
Styrofoam cups
Styrofoam square
sunlight
tables
tape
tape measure
tap water

thermometers (at least two of identical
  size)
thread
toy truck
trowel
T square
typing or computer paper
water
wind gauge
wood dowel
wood glue

INDEX

95